PURR-FECT PETS

Most cats have an independent streak, and will spend time on their own, exploring and hunting. They will head for home when they are ready to share their affections and curl up with their special humans.

TAKE ME HOME
If you choose a newborn kitten, you will have to wait until it is about twelve weeks old before it can leave its mother.

TINY THINGS
Kittens need their mother to feed them, keep them clean and safe, and teach them how to survive before they are ready to live in a new home.

DID YOU KNOW?

A kitten drinks its mother's milk until it is about six weeks old.

BORN TO BE WILD
Even pet cats have wild instincts, and hunt for small creatures.

HEALTHY HINTS

Cats can be affected by some nasty diseases. They need to be vaccinated against them when they are tiny, and again at three months old. They should not go outdoors until they have had these injections, or they may be at risk.

DID YOU KNOW?

Cats, like humans, can catch the flu. It gives them a runny nose and a sore throat.

FURRY FRIENDS

Some cats have beautifully patterned short fur, while others have luxurious long coats. A few breeds have such fine hair that they look almost bald! Cats groom themselves and love to be clean, but they will need your help to keep their coat in prime condition.

FURBALLS

Cats shed their hair all the time. At certain times they lose more than normal. A cat licks its coat to groom itself, and may swallow some fur. This gathers in its insides until the cat coughs it up as a furball. Brushing and combing their fur will help to remove loose hairs so they don't swallow as much when they keep themselves clean.

DID YOU KNOW?

Most cats prefer to be stroked and brushed in the direction of their fur, not against it.

ROUGH STUFF

A cat's tongue has hook-shaped bumps and will feel rough when it licks your hand. These bumps act like a comb to catch loose hairs, and help to remove dirt and knots in their fur.

SHORT HAIR

Long-haired cats need brushing more often than short-haired cats, but you should still groom a short-haired cat every week. It is bonding time together when your cat learns to trust you. Start when your cat is small and it will soon get used to being brushed. It is like giving your pet a massage! It improves the cat's blood circulation and skin condition as well as keeping the fur clean.

ALMOST HAIRLESS

A Sphynx cat looks hairless but actually has soft, fine hairs on its skin, like a peach. Their lack of fur can make them look bony, but they are strong and well-muscled, and weigh more than you might think.

CLASSIC CAT

One of the most beloved long-haired breeds is the Persian which was first seen over 400 years ago in the Middle East. It was taken to Europe and the USA because of their striking good looks and beautiful fur. They make great pets and love cuddles and attention, although they prefer peace and quiet rather than noise and chaos.

DID YOU KNOW?

Persian cats often have large orange eyes, although you may find some with blue or green eyes.

SHOW CATS

Many cats are mixed-breed, and they make affectionate and loving pets. However, some families go out of their way to buy a particular breed of pedigree cat because they like the way it looks and the personality that breed often shows. They may even want to take their pet to a cat show to see if it can win a prize.

BURMESE

This breed has a rounded head with medium sized ears, and often has brown fur. Its paws and nose should also be brown. They are clever creatures that can learn tricks and love company. They will get lonely if they spend all day on their own.

TURKISH VAN

A rare breed, the Turkish Van has a white body with brown or black markings on its face and tail. Unlike most cats, they really love the water and have been nicknamed "swimming cats" because of their enthusiasm for diving in!

MUNCHKIN

Can you spot anything unusual about this cat? That's right, it has exceptionally short legs! Despite this, Munchkins love to run, and are fast and full of energy. They will happily play with toys and learn tricks.

SIAMESE

If you want a chatty cat, this is the pet for you! They are well-known for making lots of noise and demanding your attention. They are nosy animals, poking into cupboards, finding new hiding places, watching TV, and following you around to see what you're doing. Siamese cats have striking blue eyes and pale fur with darker points on their face, feet, and tail.

DID YOU KNOW?

Siamese cats can be taken for walks and will play fetch, just like a pet dog!

SCOTTISH FOLD
The most striking thing about this breed is its folded ears. As a kitten, its ears stick up, but begin to bend forward as it grows up. Although the ears lie close to its head, the cat can still hear well, and moves its ears to show anger and other emotions. Scottish Folds love to sleep on their back or sit with their legs out and their paws on their stomach.

DID YOU KNOW?

Not all Scottish Folds have folded ears. Some have ears that stay straight; they are known as Scottish Shorthairs.

SLEEPING LIKE A BABY

Baby cats are called kittens, and their mothers are called queens. A queen will give birth to a handful of kittens at once, called a litter. Cats often have four to six babies in one litter, but sometimes many more. The mother is pregnant for around nine weeks, and can give birth up to five times in one year!

BLIND BABIES

When a kitten is born, its eyes are closed and its ears don't work properly. After about two weeks, its eyes open and it begins to hear sounds better. By the time it is four weeks old it can walk without falling, and soon it will be running, jumping, and playing with its brothers and sisters.

DID YOU KNOW?

The biggest litter of kittens on record is 19, although only 15 of them survived.

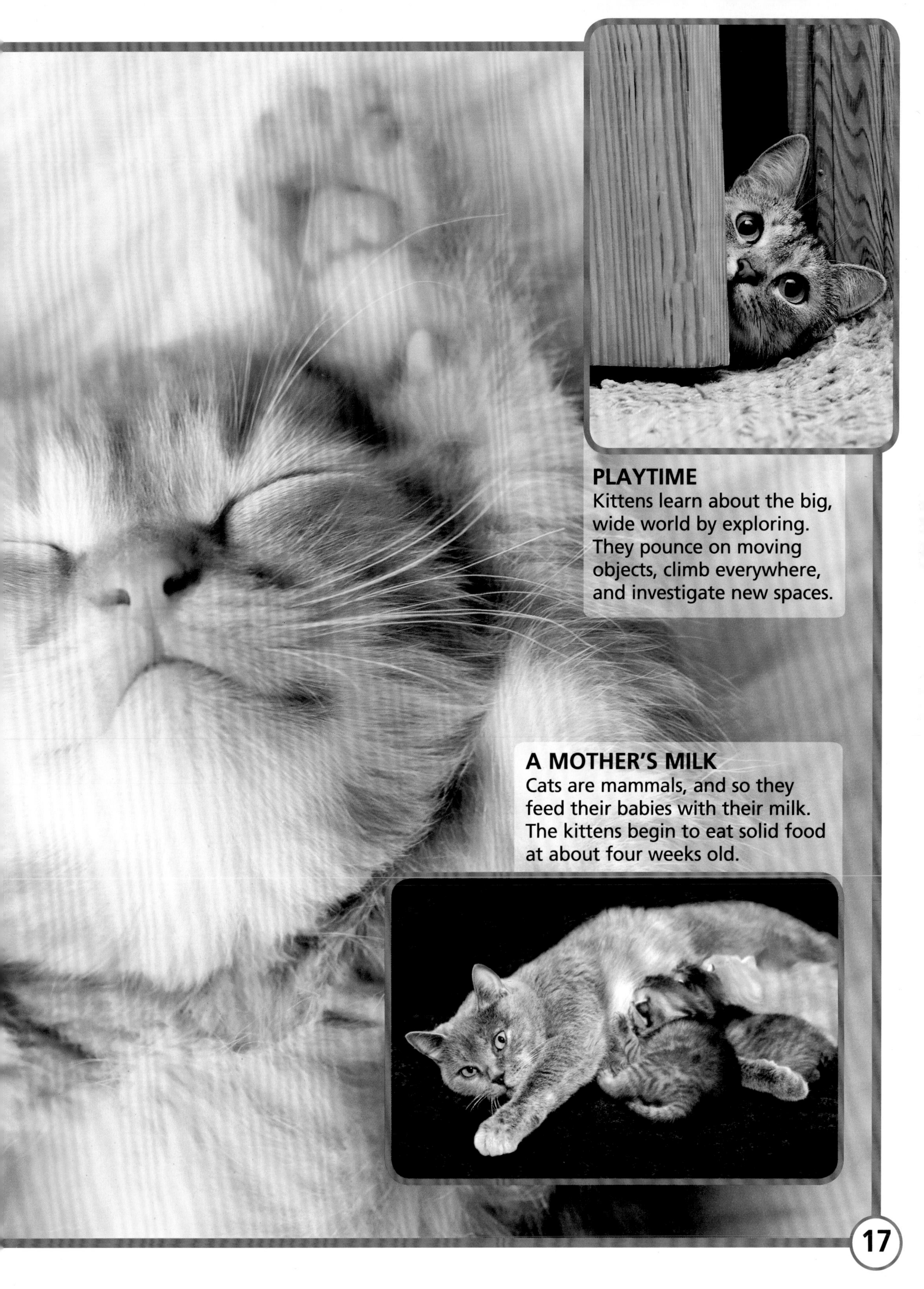

PLAYTIME

Kittens learn about the big, wide world by exploring. They pounce on moving objects, climb everywhere, and investigate new spaces.

A MOTHER'S MILK

Cats are mammals, and so they feed their babies with their milk. The kittens begin to eat solid food at about four weeks old.

CATS' EYES

When a kitten's eyes first open, they will be blue. Some cats keep these blue eyes as adults, but many change as the kitten gets older. Cats can have bright gold or yellow eyes, green or pale copper, but unlike humans their eyes never become dark brown.

DID YOU KNOW?

Some cats have eyes that don't match. This is most often seen in pure white cats.

EYES AND EARS

Cats are designed for hunting, even if their loving owners put out food in a bowl every day. Their body has super senses for tracking down prey, and sharp teeth and claws for catching it.

FEELING THE WAY

A cat has extra long, thick hairs on its face called whiskers. These are extremely sensitive, and help it to feel its way around, even in the dark. The whiskers can also pick up small movements in the air if a mouse is scuttling past.

SUPER SNIFFER

A cat's nose is much more sensitive than the nose of a human. It helps the cat to track down its food, even at night or if it is stalking a moving creature.

DID YOU KNOW?

The longest whiskers on a cat's face are the same width as the cat's body to help it judge spaces.

SUPER SENSE

Hearing is extremely important for hunting, both day and night. A cat's ears act like satellite dishes to pick up tiny noises. The earflaps have lots of muscles to swivel around and catch sounds from all directions.

BRIGHT EYES

A cat has oval pupils in the middle of its eyes that open to let in more light when the cat hunts at night. These pupils narrow to slits to keep out bright lights. They can adjust very quickly to help a cat see well. Cats' eyes have an extra layer inside to help them see in low light. It acts like a mirror to reflect light, and makes a cat's eyes glow in car headlights if you see them at night.

BALANCING ACT

Cats have a superb sense of balance that allows them to walk confidently along a narrow fence, or climb along a swaying tree branch. Their tail acts like a stabilizer to stop them from wobbling, and they have special sections inside their ears to keep them upright. Cats are famous for landing on their feet if they fall. Their ears help them tell which way up they need to be, and their super-bendy spine twists so their feet are the first thing to hit the ground.

DID YOU KNOW?

A cat can jump around five times its own height!

WILD THINGS

Your pet cat may love to curl up on your bed or climb onto your knee and be stroked, but at heart it is a wild animal, designed to hunt small creatures to keep itself alive. Cats that are allowed to roam outdoors still stalk birds and mice, and might sometimes even bring back their prey to show you!

LIVING TOGETHER

Cats and dogs can live happily in the same family, especially if they have grown up together from when they were tiny. Keeping smaller pets, however, can be tricky, as your cat's natural instinct is to chase it and grab it. Just watch your cat leap on a toy on a string and you will see how quickly it can pounce!

DID YOU KNOW?

Cats are one of the only living creatures to survive on a meat-only diet.

WHO GOES THERE?

The slightest twitch in the grass will attract your cat's attention. It will focus all its senses on finding out if there is something hiding that is worth eating.

BABY HUNTER

A kitten learns how to hunt by watching its mother and playing with other kittens. They follow their mother's tail as it flicks from side to side, and squash themselves low to the ground before pouncing.

SILENT STALKER

A hunting cat takes slow, silent steps to creep up on its prey. When it gets close enough, it uses its strong back legs to push itself forward in a fast, giant leap.

HUNTERS THROUGH HISTORY

The hunting skills of a cat were what first made them appealing to humans. Cats were useful for killing the rats that lived near human food stores and ate all of the grain. People took them into their home, kept them warm, and gave them a safe place to breed. Many centuries later, humans still keep cats as pets, and cats still hunt small creatures!

DID YOU KNOW?

Adult cats have strong, sharp teeth for hunting, but a kitten's tiny teeth are even sharper, like needles!

HOUSE CATS

Many people keep their cat indoors all the time. A cat can spend many hours sleeping, but it will need something to keep it occupied when it is awake. Make sure it has plenty of toys to play with.

HIDE AND SEEK

Cats are nosy creatures. They hate to see a space and not know what is inside! Their hunting instincts tell them to explore everything, from the top of the kitchen cabinet to interesting boxes and laundry baskets!

MINI HUNTERS

Kittens learn how to hunt by playing with toys. They will often grab an item and pass it between their front paws or kick it around with their back feet.

DID YOU KNOW?

Kittens lose their baby teeth, just like humans do, and it's not unusual to find tiny teeth caught in the things they were chewing while they played!

SHINY THINGS

Moving objects could be prey, and so cats are attracted to them. They often love shiny things as they glimmer with reflected light, which makes the cat sit up and take notice. Nothing is safe from a cat's inquisitive paws!

RAZOR SHARP

Cats are armed with a super-sharp claw on each toe. They use them to climb, protect themselves, and to pin items to the ground. Each claw fits into a pocket of skin and can be pulled inward to keep them off the ground. This allows your cat to stalk silently, and prevents the claws becoming blunt when they walk on hard ground.

DID YOU KNOW?

Cats don't walk on their whole foot like humans do, but tiptoe on the front part only.

FUN IN THE SUN

Most cats love to find a sunny spot for a snooze. They can often be found curled up in a warm place, soaking up the rays. Indoor cats are safe to sleep wherever they like, but careful cats will only sleep outdoors if they feel free from danger.

HIGHER AND HIGHER

Cats are excellent climbers, and can scramble quickly up a tree to chase a bird or escape from a threat. Their sharp claws allow them to grip securely. Coming back down is more tricky, and they usually make their way down in reverse, much more slowly!

DID YOU KNOW?

A cat can run really fast – much faster than a human. It can sprint for short distances at up to 30 mph, the same speed as a car on a city road.

KEEP AWAY

Cats that live together often fight as part of their playtime. However, a cat will attack a stranger if it wanders into its own space. They hiss and flatten their ears to show they mean business.

CAT NAPPING

When a cat has explored and played, it needs to sleep to repower its energy stores. Sleeping in the sunshine is a good way to recharge its batteries!

OUT AND ABOUT

If your pet is allowed outdoors, be aware that some plants are poisonous to cats. Certain houseplants are dangerous too, so seek advice on which ones to keep out of your home. They can damage your cat's organs, or irritate their skin and mouth.

DID YOU KNOW?

You may notice your pet eating grass, but don't be alarmed. It helps their digestion and gives them vitamins. Sometimes they eat enough to make them vomit on purpose, to clear out feathers, furs, bones, and even parasites they have swallowed while hunting.

CAT NAPS

NOSY PETS

One of the reasons cats are so nosy is that they're trying to find a safe place to curl up and sleep. Even the most unlikely spots might be appealing to your pet!

ON THE PROWL

Cats do much of their hunting at the start and end of the night, when their prey is active. They spend a lot of the daytime fast asleep.

CATS AND DOGS

It is possible for a cat and dog to be friends, especially if they grow up together from a young age.

Pet cats have many similar habits to their wild relatives. They use a lot of energy hunting in short bursts, and then spend the rest of their time cleaning themselves and sleeping. Cats take a nap several times a day, and sleep for twice as long as humans do – around 15 hours every day!

DID YOU KNOW?

Kittens and really old cats sleep even more than young to middle-aged cats.

HALF AWAKE

Even though they sleep for hours, only a small fraction of that time is spent in deep sleep. The rest of the time, your cat is only dozing, possibly with one eye almost open, so it knows what is going on around it. They are ready to leap into action if they hear a noise or sense danger.

DID YOU KNOW?

A cat's tummy is the most vulnerable place on its body. If it rolls onto its back, it shows it feels safe and trusts you. Even so, tickle its head, not its tummy.

BIG CATS

That tiny kitten you fell in love with will grow into a larger adult – but not as big as its wild relatives! Cheetahs, lions, tigers, jaguars, and leopards are all closely related to your pet, with many similar characteristics.

CAT SNACKS

To keep your cat happy and healthy, try not to give him snacks in between meals. In the wild, cats can go relatively long periods of time without food.

SEE THE SIGNS

Cats have their own territory, or space to roam. They make scratch marks to show other cats to stay away.

CLEAN MACHINE

After a cat has killed and eaten, it needs to get clean. They hate to have blood or mud on their paws and fur.

DID YOU KNOW?

Many big cats can roar, but they cannot purr like a small cat. A cheetah purrs rather than roaring, despite its size.

CARRYING HER CUBS

A wild cat, such as a lioness or cheetah, has to keep her tiny cubs safe from other predators. She will often move them from place to place to stay ahead of her enemies. She picks each cub up in her mouth, holding the loose skin behind its head. Domestic cats still do the same, even though they live in a much safer world.

DID YOU KNOW?
A kitten stays perfectly still and keeps its legs and tail tucked in so that it is easier for it to be carried.

SAY WHAT?

Cats make a huge range of noises – many more than dogs can make. They have at least 100 sounds to show humans how they're feeling and to communicate with other cats. They also use body language to get their message across.

AN UNHAPPY CAT

Growling, hissing, spitting, and baring its teeth are signs that your cat is unhappy and on guard. It is a warning to stay away.

DID YOU KNOW?

A cat purrs when it is happy, but also if it is sick. It is thought that the purring helps to make them feel better.

FLUFF IT UP

Many creatures fluff up their fur or feathers if they are in danger. It makes them look bigger and scarier, so they are less likely to be attacked. Cats do this, as well as arching their back high in the air.

NOISY CREATURES

Kittens make a lot of noise as they learn to express how they are feeling, and have a lot of new things to "talk" about!

SAY HELLO

Humans shake hands or fist bump when they meet, but cats often rub noses to say hi.

DID YOU KNOW?

Cats flick their tail from side to side when they are watching something they would like to pounce on.

BABY NOISES

Kittens meow a lot more than adult cats do. It is their way of letting their mother know where they are, and that they need her attention, even when they are tiny and their eyes are shut tight.

BEST FRIENDS

It is often said that a man's best friend is his dog, but cats make excellent companions. They don't need to be taken for walks, they eat much less than many dogs, and they take a lot less space in your home! A healthy, well-looked after cat can live for more than 20 years, keeping you company with lots of cuddles.

TOP CAT
The Maine Coon is one of the largest cat breeds, with a long, silky coat. It can grow as large as a human toddler!

ANCIENT PETS
Cats were kept in houses in Egypt thousands of years ago. They were considered so special they were made into mummies when they died!

NO TAIL
Most cats use their tail for balance, but some breeds manage perfectly well without. Manx cats and Bobtails have just a stump or a small, fluffy tuft.

BAD NEWS?
Black cats have long been associated with witches, but in some countries they are thought to bring good luck if they cross your path.